Hans in Luck

Written by Paeony Lewis

Illustrated by Andrés Martínez Ricci

OXFORD
UNIVERSITY PRESS

Long ago, Hans set out to visit his mum.

It was hot on the road and Hans had a big bag of silver.

"He looks quick," said Hans.

"You can have him for the bag of silver," said the man.

"What luck!" said Hans.

But Hans fell off!

There was a farmer with a cow.
"I like milk," said Hans.

"You can have my cow if I can have him," said the farmer.
"What luck!" said Hans.

But the cow had no milk.

Hans met a man with a chicken.
He said, "You can have my chicken."
"What luck!" said Hans. "I like eggs."

But Hans got a peck.

Hans met a miller with a big mill rock and a little mill rock.

"What luck!" said Hans. "I will have some buns."

But the rocks fell in a deep pond.

With no rocks, Hans was now quick.

So Hans said, "Mum! I had good luck."

Retell the story

Once upon a time...

The end.